COLORS DIVIDED CANNOT BE UNITED

Lisa Rucker Butler

Written By
Lisa Rucker Butler
Copyright 2021

MIDNIGHT MOON
BOOKS
CLEVELAND, OHIO
Illustrations
Lisa Rucker Butler
ISBN: 9798715442208

2

TABLE OF CONTENTS

INTRODUCTION

IN THE BEGINNING,
THERE WERE NO COLORS.
THE UNIVERSE WAS GLOOM,
WITH NO FLOWERS TO BLOOM.

WE NEED COLORS, LIKE BALLOONS.

LIKE OUR CREATOR SAID,
"LET THERE BE LIGHT."
HE MADE EVERYTHING IN SIGHT.
LIKE COLORS,
LET US UNITE.

LIKE OUR CREATOR
MADE DIFFERENT FACES.
I WILL START WITH
THE BASICS,
OF COLORS; YELLOW, BLUE
AND RED,
LET US LEARN FROM
THE PAGES
AHEAD.

BASIC COLORS

YELLOW, BLUE, AND RED

CHAPTER 1

<u>YELLOW</u>

SOME OF OUR DAYS CAN BE LIKE <u>LEMONS</u>.
EVEN STILL, WE SHOULD RESPECT OUR
FELLOW,
MEN,
LIKE THE <u>SUNRAYS</u>,
ARE VERY BRIGHT,
LET US NOT FIGHT.
OUR SOULS AND SPIRITS TOGETHER,
SHOULD BE
MELLOW.
YELLOW

BLUE

WHO KNEW?
OUR COUNTRY WOULD BE SIDED.
RED OR BLUE,
LIKE THE RED SEA DIVIDED,
THEN AGAIN UNITED,
FOR THE FREE.
THEIR LIVES WERE SWEET AS BLUEBERRIES.
WE SHOULD BE FREE FROM PAIN,
LIKE NON-SYRINGED VEINS.
TODAY I AM SO SAD I COULD CRY.
FEELING BLUE,
I SIGH.
LET US AIM TOGETHER HIGH,
TO THE SKY.
FOR ALL COLORFUL BALLOONS
TO FLY.
TOGETHER
EVER AND EVER.

RED

ANGER AND RAGE,
ENOUGH SAID.
BE GLAD TO WAKE UP OUT THE BED,
TO SEE ANOTHER DAY.
THE DAY ANEW,
FLOWING LIKE WATER,
LIKE BLOOD,
LIKE THE FLOOD,
WITH NOAH'S ARK.
LET US NOT BE A PART.
LIKE RED ROSES, THEIR BEAUTY,
LET US LIVE IN UNITY.
LIKE LOVE, SWEET AS CHERRIES,
OUR SOULS NEED FED,
NOT BURIED LIKE THE DEAD.
DRIED BLOOD TO LEAVE OUR LOVE ONES TO DREAD,
FROM ANGER THAT LED
TO DANGER.
RED

Colors United

CHAPTER 2

YELLOW+RED=ORANGE

LIKE THE DAY WE WERE BORN,
FROM DOMESTIC TO FOREIGN.
WE WAS GIVEN THE GIFT OF LIFE.
MOST PARENTS TAUGHT THEIR CHILDREN TO TREAT
OTHERS RIGHT.
LET US UNITE,
NOT FIGHT,
NOT DIVDED,
LIKE PUMPKIN HALVES.
WE NEED TO HAVE CHARACTER OF MERIT.
LIKE THE AGE OF YOUNG CALVES,
FRESH AS CARROTS,
PICKED FROM THE GROUND.
LET US NOT LET OUR COUNTRY GO DOWN.

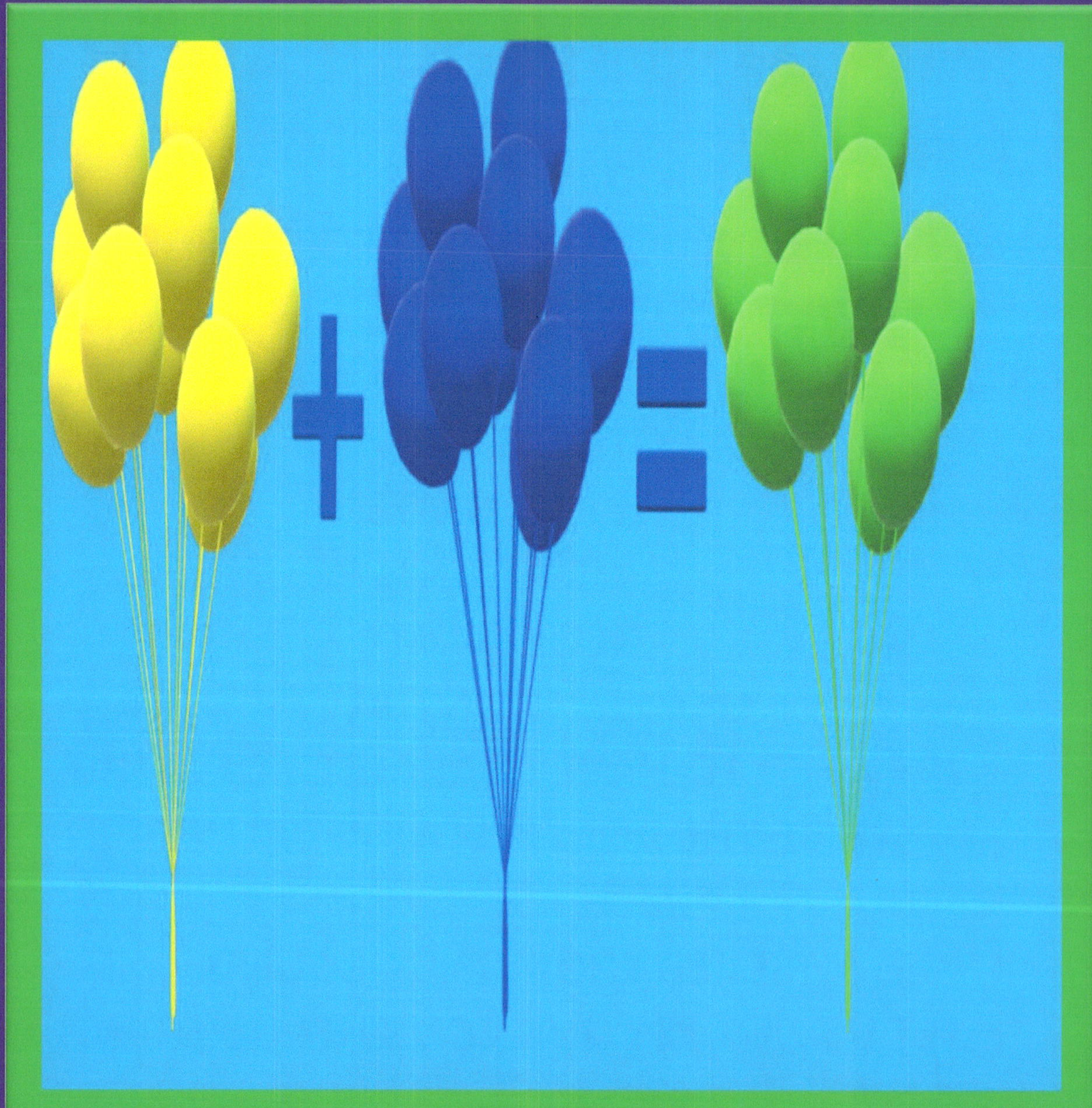

YELLOW+BLUE=GREEN
AS GREEN AS THE LEAVES,
WE ARE HUMAN BEINGS.
SWEET AS PEAS ,
WE SHOULD BE,
NOT LIKE THIS WORLD SO MEAN.
WITH HARDLY ANY SHOULDERS TO LEAN.
LIKE UNSALTED GREEN BEANS,
HEALTHY.
PEOPLE ARE PREJUDGED BY BEING POOR
OR WEALTHY.
LIKE BRUSSEL SPROUTS,
LETS WORK OUR DIFFERENCES
OUT.

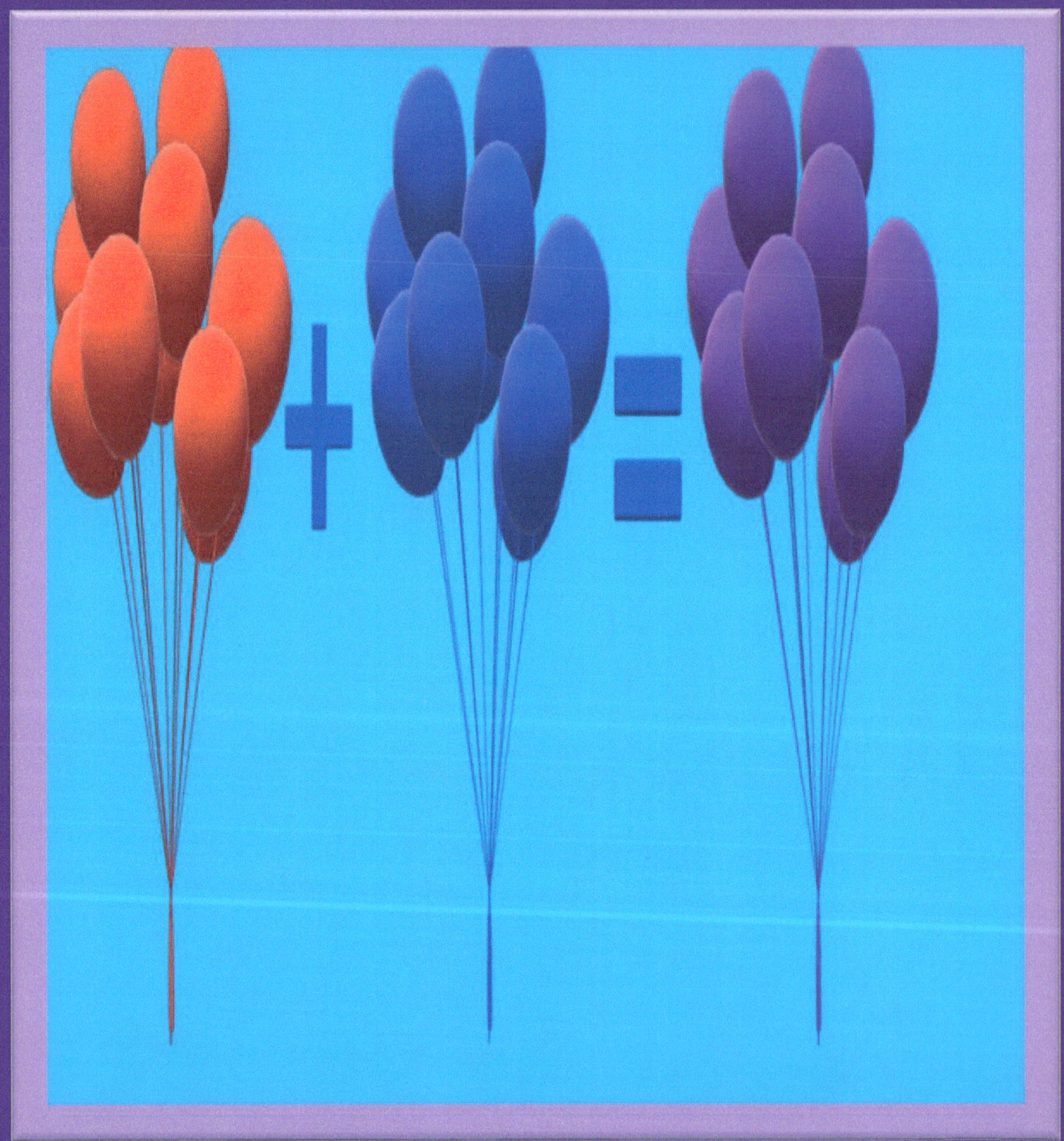

RED+BLUE=PURPLE

SWEET AS <u>GRAPES,</u>
FOR GOODNESS SAKE,
WHY SHOULD WE HATE,
OTHERS BECAUSE OF THEIR RACE,
SUCH DISGRACE
OR HATE BECAUSE OF THEIR POLITICAL PARTY,
BITTERSWEET LIKE THE <u>PLUM.</u>
LET US NOT BE THE VICTUMS
OF GENERATIONS CONTINUING THIS CIRCLE.
PURPLE

BEYOND THE
BASICS
CHAPTER 3

WHITE

HARD AS <u>SUGAR CUBES</u>
ON OTHERS THAT ARE DIFFERENT THAN YOU.
TO SOFT AS SILK,
NOT COLD LIKE <u>MILK.</u>
TOGETHER WE CAN BUILD.
CREATOR WOULD BE THRILLED.
NOT ALL IS THIS WAY
THANKS FOR LOVING
THE HUMAN RACE.

BLACK

LIKE <u>BLACK LICORICE,</u>
NOT LIKED BY MOST.
TOSSED OUT LIKE <u>BURNT TOAST</u>
BECAUSE OF ITS FLAVOR.
YOU ARE NOT LIKED BECAUSE
OF YOUR DIFFERENCE.
YOU ARE TIRED OF THESE
PERDICUMENTS.
JUST LIKE IN THE MINES,
WHICH IS FULL OF <u>COALS.</u>
YOU CAN ACCOMPLISH YOUR
GOALS.
WITH OTHER COLORS,
SISTERS AND BROTHERS
OF ANOTHER MOTHER.

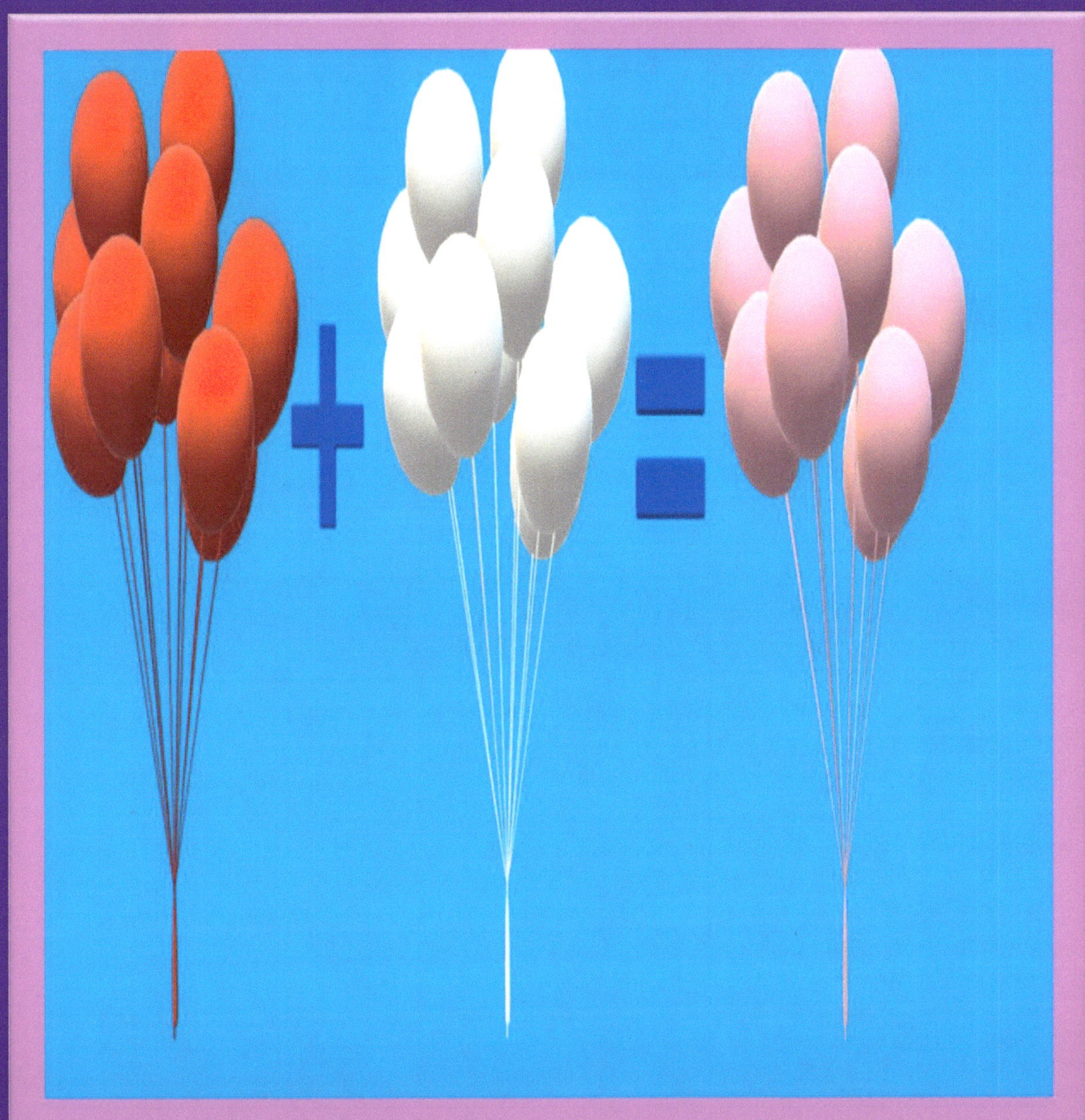

PINK

THE WORLD CAN BE DIRTY LIKE THE PIG,
TRYING TO HAVE SOME DIRT TO DIG.
FULL OF GREED,
HATING SOMEONE BECAUSE OF RACE OR CREED.
TRYING TO HURT ONE ANOTHER,
DESTROYING YOUR SISTER OR BROTHER.
WITH THE FLAPPING OF LIPS,
THOSE EVIL TONGUES,
CAN CAUSE AN ETHNIC OR POLITICAL GROUPS'
REPUTATION TO BE
DONE.
EVIL DONE UNDER THE SUN,
LIKE A BOOMERANG,
CAN COME BACK TO YOU WITH A BANG.
LIKE EYELID WITH A BLINK,
BEFORE YOU SPEAK
YOU SHOULD THINK.
PINK

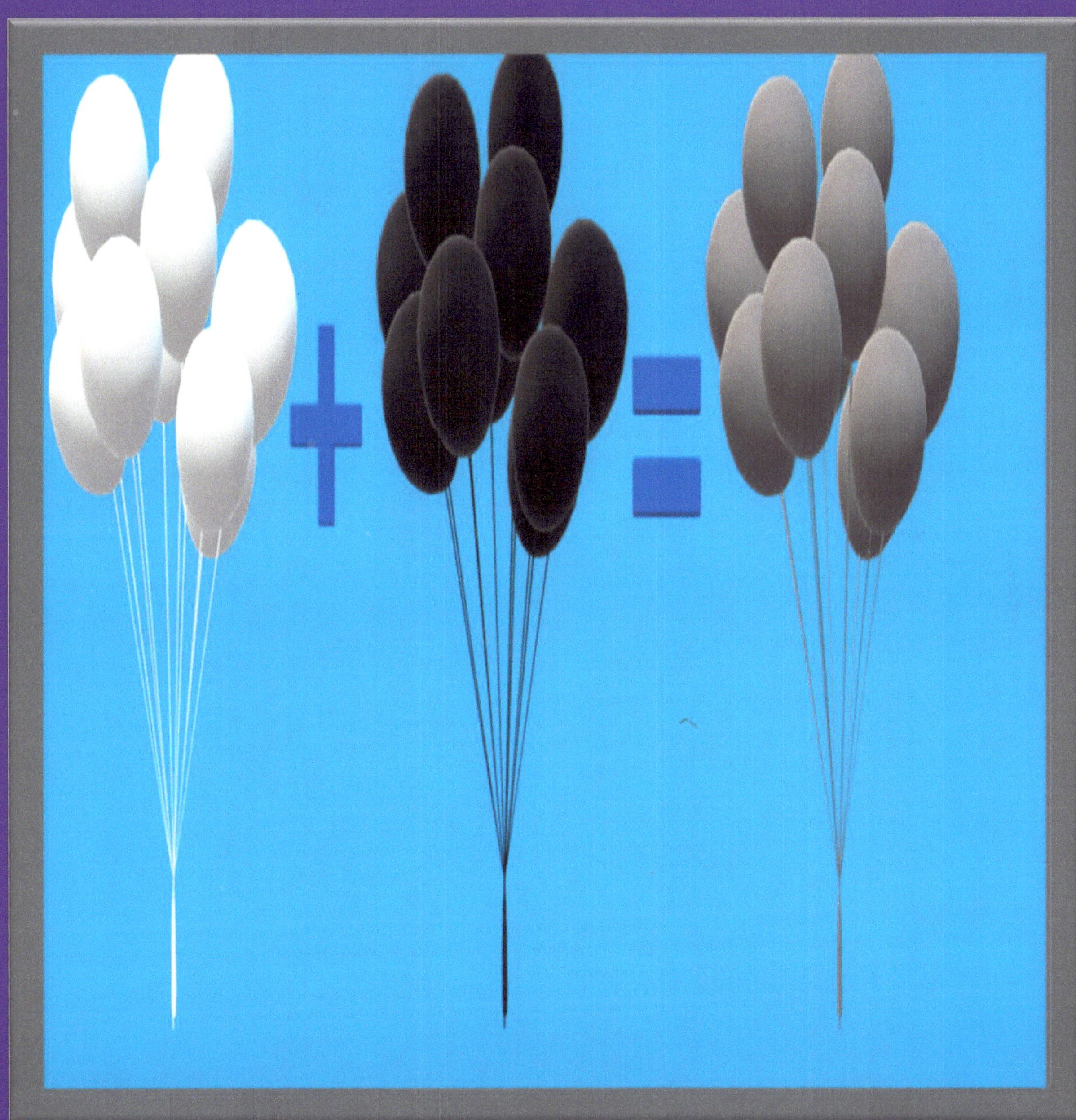

WHITE+BLACK=GREY

TWO RIVALS COME TOGETHER,
LOOPED LIKE THE CHAIN,
LIKE THE RAIN
AND SUN,
COMING TOGETHER AS ONE.
LIKE PUTTING DOWN OUR GUNS,
HAVING THE BEST OF BOTH WORLDS,
LIKE CHOCOLATE AND VANILLA SWIRL,
PRECIOUS LIKE A PEARL.
HAVING TO CHOOSE IN THIS WORLD,
ON WHICH CULTURE TO SIDE,
WILL KEEP US WITH DIVIDE.
LIKE DIVISION,
THE MEDIA ON THE TELEVISON,
LET US THINK A NEW WAY.
THIS IS A NEW DAY.

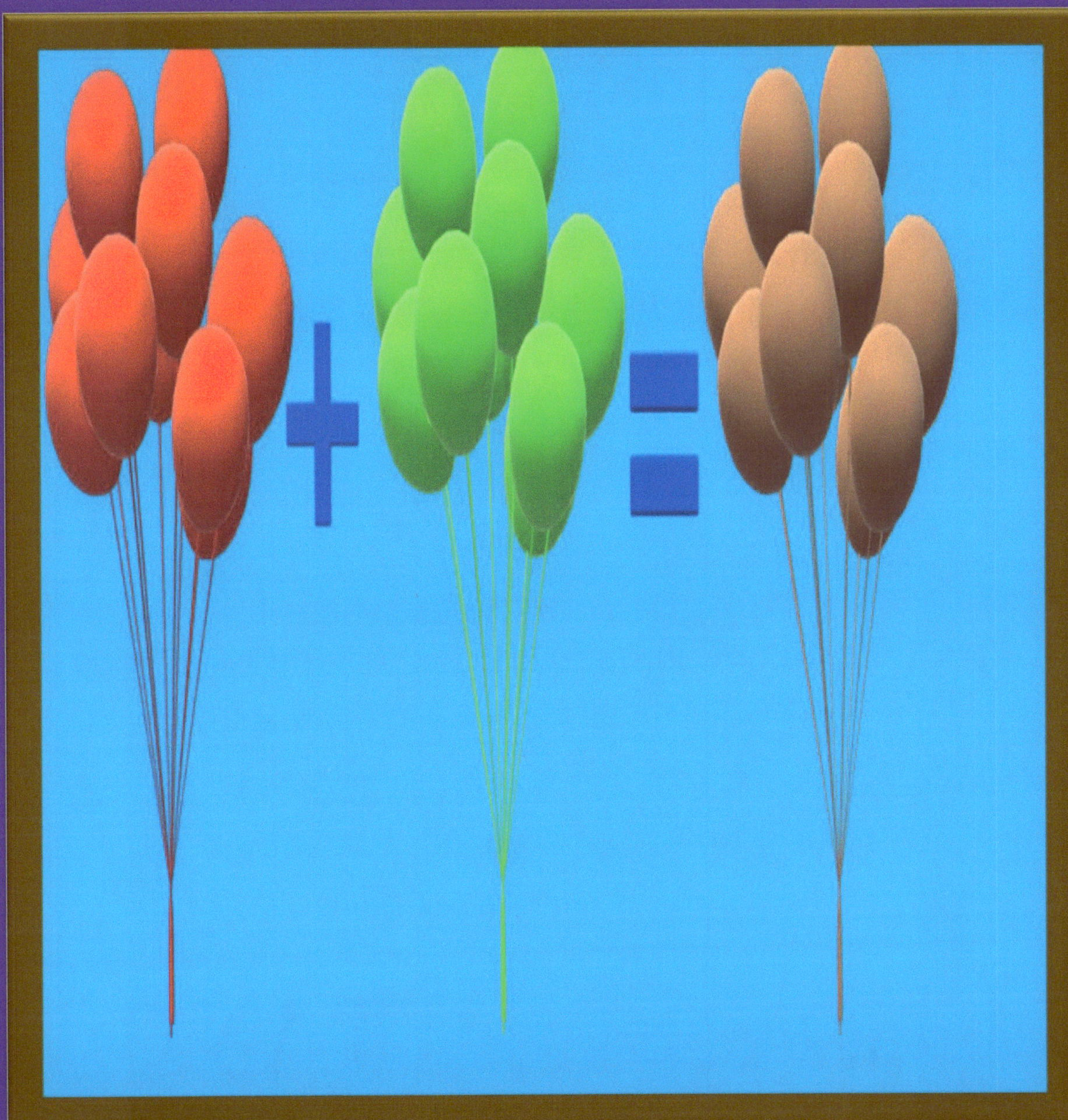

GREEN+RED=BROWN

FROM OLD COUNTRY TO TOWN,
SOME WORKING FOR <u>PENNIES,</u>
DOLLAR BILLS ADDED SAVED
IS MANY.
SOME MAY FROWN,
OTHERS FEELING JOBS ARE TAKEN,
STOP MISTAKEN,
STOP HATING.
THERE ARE PLENTY OPPORTUNITIES TO GO AROUND.
SOME DAYS MAY GET YOU DOWN,
REMAINING SWEET & SOLID LIKE A <u>CHOCOLATE</u> <u>CANDY BAR,</u>
BEING PROUD OF WHO YOU ARE.
TOGETHER WE CAN WORK HARD AS WE CAN,

UNITED WE STAND.

FLYING HIGH AHEAD

CHAPTER 4

FLYING HIGH AHEAD

WHETHER YOU ARE RED, WHITE, BLACK, YELLOW OR
BROWN,
LET US NOT LET OUR CREATOR DOWN.
WITH THE FROWNS,
OF JUDGEMENT OF SOMEONE'S SKIN,
DON'T YOU KNOW THAT IS A SIN.
WITH SIN YOU CAN'T WIN,
THE ADVERSARY CAN BREAK IN.
BREAKING OUR COUNTRY DOWN,
BECAUSE HE HATES,
HIS MISSION IS TO DESTROY THE HUMAN RACE.

JUST LIKE A VIRUS,
HE DO NOT DISCRIMINATE.
LET US GET BEYOND THE ADVERSARY'S PLAN,
TO LOVE OUR FELLOW MAN.
WE CAN UNITE,
AND NOT FIGHT,
SO WE CAN AIM HIGH,
TOGETHER WE CAN FLY.
IF WE LIVE RIGHT
ON EARTH AND NOT SEVER,
WE WILL UNITE GOING BEYOND THE STARS,
FAR,
LIKE BALLOONS,
FOREVER AND EVER.
LET US NOT FIGHT AGAIN,
LET US MAKE AMENDS,
AMEN.

THANKS AND PRAISES

TO HEAVENLY FATHER GOD FOR GIVING ME THIS IDEA TO CREATE THIS BOOK.

Hebrews 13:1 KJV
Let brotherly love continue.

SHOUT OUTS

SHOUT OUTS TO MY FAMILY, MY HUSBAND DOUGLAS EARL BUTLER, SONS JEFFREY JAMES FORD III, XAVIER ALLEN FORD, AND JOHN THOMAS OREFICE AND TO MY DAUGHTER JALISA VALENTINA OREFICE

ABOUT THE AUTHOR

Lisa Rucker Butler

Is an Independent Author. She has co-written "How To Defeat Satan", with husband Douglas Earl Butler. Lisa has been a Christian for many years and is inspired to right non-fiction and fiction to target all ages for promoting humanity with Christianity.

www.ingramcontent.com/pod-product-compliance
Lightning Source LLC
Chambersburg PA
CBHW040150240726
48664CB00002B/651